# Three Steps to Family

### *Realign, Reconnect,*

### *Grow together.*

## By David and Laura Helen

Aka Daddy and Mummy.

Also Available by Forever Family

# Money for Kids

By Tegan Helen

# Power to Unlock your Dreams

By Tegan Helen

3 Steps to family
By David and Laura Helen

First published 2016 by 831 Designs
Foreverfamilyforeverfree.com

ISBN-13: 978-1541378926

ISBN-10: 154137892X

WARNING - DISCLAIMER

Forever Family Forever Free has designed this book to provide information in regard to the subject matter covered. It is sold with the understanding that the authors are not liable for the misconception or misuse of information provided. Every effort has been made to make this guide as complete and as accurate as possible. The authors shall have neither liability nor responsibility to any person or entity with respect to any loss, damage or injury caused or alleged to be caused directly or indirectly by the information contained in this book.

Second Place
2nd
Huge Congratulations!
Dan! woohoo!
Great effort,

love your concept,

excited to start

working with you!

love David + Laura
Helen
xx

# Dedication

We would Love to thank our beautiful children.
Tegan Helen our inspiring author and Tyler
David our inventor.
It is you two that inspire us to be the best
parents that we can be, and to show us the true
meaning of unconditional love.
We learn so much from your beautiful souls and
open hearts.

Far as a star
Xxxx 831 xxxX

We would also Love to thank Matt Maddix and
Joseph Giglietti for their amazing "Jump start
your book" programme, and the inspiration to
write our book.

# Three Steps to Family

# Table of Contents

******Bonus Section******

# Endorsements

*"Laura, David, Tegan and Tyler as a family they have incredible, amazing values and beliefs. They are a family that are going to reach millions of lives."*

*- Warren Inspire Ryan - Fearless Speaking Academy & The Mind Mechanic*

*"I've learnt many things in life and one of the most profound was the ability to love someone unconditionally. I'm reminded of that when I watch Laura with her family.*

*There is a bond which you can see has been nurtured over time with care and attention. In a busy world where distractions are abundant, Laura has the ability to refocus you on the things in life which really matter."*

*- Steve Woody - #1 International Bestseller Founder of Online Mastery*

*"In this book, David and Laura have provided millions of families with three ultra special gifts - Alignment, Connection and Growth.*

*I remember starting one of my earlier companies thinking, man, having a business AND a family is super hard!*

*I also realised that one you can start again - business, the other you can't - family.*

*In fact, I learned early on that in order to have a successful business and be the best entrepreneur I could be, that being aligned, connected and growing with my family was essential!*

*David and Laura have shared some amazing stories about the ups and downs of their family life and how that turned into successes for them.*

*This book will give you some great activities you can do on day one and ideas that can be used to inspire us all to grow together as a family."*

*- Julian 'The Ultrapreneur' Hall*

*I met this family previously and I haven't met such a joyful and caring family . It's amazing to see how they take part in things together and are always caring for their loved ones . They're always supporting everyone . What I like about this family the most is that they're one of a kind family . You won't ever meet another family like this and that's what will take them to the top . Keep on loving each other and care for others!*

*- Inspiring Vanessa*

## Foreword

*Having heard about the amazing and inspiring Tegan
and her story, I had the pleasure to meet Laura & David
at a Self Development event in London where Tegan and
my little boys were speaking on stage. Laura and David
are such inspirational parents, human beings with
beautiful souls. They are an excellent example of
amazing parenting which shows in Tegan and her little
brother Tyler. As a parent , I was blown away seeing
Tegan speaking on stage and being an author of two
books! A friend and an international world class speaker
Ashley Zahabian told me on the way to the airport that
she couldn't believe that at a 7 y.o. knows about
"compound interest". All the credit goes to the parents,
as without them Tegan would not be where she is now,
and inspiring other children to think outside the box and
do what they love. I call this amazing parenting that
allows their children to BE and express themselves
beautifully, guiding them in life, allowing them to fly and
grow and just being the support behind their children's
wings. "*

*- Alicia Borta, Mindset Coach &
Speaker*

# Three Steps to Family

# Open Your Heart
# Open Your Mind

# Three Steps to Family

# Step One

# Realign.

*"Everyone needs a house to live in, but a supportive family is what builds a home." -Anthony Liccione*

In the beginning of our story as a family, both David and I were trying to make a bad situation better. We were both trying so hard to make life good for us all. I had my couple of businesses. David had his businesses as well as a full time job. I was also a full-time stay-at-home mummy who also home-schooled the kids. We both had a lot going on. We both were doing our best to make the best for our family. We were both getting nowhere fast. We then realized we weren't setting goals. We weren't focused. We weren't aligned. We didn't really know where we were going. Our goal and dream was to just have "more." To just have enough money that, if the washing machine broke, life doesn't come to a halt and we have to figure out how to solve that issue.

I'm going to use an analogy we recently heard and love from Garrain Jones, which is "life is like driving a car with no GPS" So, you punch the co-ordinates into the GPS and, if you follow the instructions the GPS gives you, you're going to arrive at your destination. If however you do not put your destination (your goals and your dreams), into the GPS, you can end up anywhere, anywhere in the world apart from where you wanted to go. The slightest thing can sidetrack you, send you off course. We've had a few other businesses that we've dipped in and out of, we started thinking, "Oh, yeah, that's cool we can make this work for us." But then we just got distracted by the noise out there. Because we had such a vague dream of, we just wanted to do "better" instead of having a focused, specific and an aligned goal.

As soon as we set our goals, as soon as we got really specific and detail crazy, we started to get somewhere, and it really started to move. When we came together as a family and wrote down all our goals together and then put all that into a bigger goal, things started happening. They started happening fast. We were all aligned. We all knew where each other was going. We all knew why each other were doing the things we were doing. We weren't driving each other crazy, not knowing why they're always busy but not with us. Why he's always busy and stressed. We finally started to understand each other. Before, we just didn't understand what each other was doing. We were all trying so hard, too hard. But, because none of us understood or listened to each other, to see what it was we were trying to do, (we didn't even know ourselves what we were trying to do). So, we were literally… if we were in that car, we'd have been driving in circles and zigzags and every which way with no actual destination because we did not know the destination, know where we were going.

*"A family is a place where minds come in contact with one another."*

**Realign, Reconnect, Grow together.    19**

So **step one, realign,** is going to get you back on track, get you guys focused as a team, as a family. Realign, you need to set your goals and dreams together so you have a destination to put into that GPS, so you guys can head straight there together, keeping each other driven and focused. When everyone understands the process and the dream, it is a lot easier to then support one another.

When we say realign, we mean get everyone on the same page. Get everyone focused on the same goals. Or not even the same goals, just all know where each other's heading, so you can understand each other support and help each other. If you don't have that destination, you're going to be all over the place. You get stressed at each other. You're getting tired. You're all working so hard and you don't even know what you're working for. It needs to be clear. You need to have that clarity on your goals so you can work together as a team and really understand each other.

**Is this book for you?**

I think it's within everyone. We all have it in us to be truly great parents. If you don't want to be a great parent, throw this book away. Don't read any more. I'm just wasting your time. When we decided to have kids we were going all in. We wanted to be the best parents we could be. That's how we've lived life. We have to be the best at what we are. And with your kids, you only get one shot at this. You can't go, "Oo, I messed up. Let's start that again." Like you can with a bad recipe or a business. The kids, once they've grown, that's it. They're up. They're gone. You only have one shot at being the best parent YOU can be. So, if that's you, if you want to be the best parent that you can be, then, yes, this book's for you. If you're not that bothered, do not read any further.

Realigning really helped us. It's like I said previously. We were all over the place. We knew we wanted a life that was better for our kids and our family but we didn't have any set goals. We weren't aiming for anything. We just wanted "better." We wanted "more." We weren't focused. As soon as we aligned ourselves and we set proper, specific goals, the only way was up. The only way was forward. We broke down our goals into sections. We started at our goal, where we want to be and worked backwards. We made it into bite-sized chunks and steps so we were able to follow through and create the life that we desire. Allowing us to focus, and to be the best parents that we can be. Without aligning, we'd still be zigzagging all over the place with no true destination.

**How would this help me and my family?**

The same way it helped us. If you find that you're working really, really hard and you get annoyed when you think you're wasting money, or your wife goes out on a shopping spree because she's stressed or your husband goes out with the guys from work because he's stressed, all these are wasting money, as the entrepreneur or the business owner of the family you may find no one else in the house gets its? Your actions are not understood. If you're both working hard as parents and not having the time to commit to your family, you CAN still get connected. This is going to help you guys. You can all get realigned and all know where each other is heading, the peace this creates within a family, when you all understand each other, when you all know what page you're on, it's such a peaceful outcome. It strengthens your family and you're able to help and support each other.

When you create this within your family you are going to receive what you focus on, you are going to build some real momentum, together. What is more powerful than a family that can head out towards their goals together knowing they've got the full support of each and every member behind them. Even if they don't quite get why other  members want it, they know their family is behind them no matter what. That is priceless; that is so powerful as a family.

## How can I implement it?

What we did, as a family, we all went away. We all created our own goals or dream boards or vision boards. Whatever term you'd like to use. We went away, created our goals, created our dreams. We got clear, on our own, what we wanted to do. What our dreams were, what our goals were. We did it all by ourselves to start with. (well we helped our little man as he is four) We all had that clarity of what life would look like, what our business would be, our home life would be, and our health and we just put it all out there, individually.

When we had completed that, we all sat around together and shared our passions one at a time. No one spoke apart from the person sharing. Which was so important because everyone felt heard. When we went through all these, we then collaborated all our ideas together to see where we all wanted to be and we all had input. I mean we've got a four and a seven year old. Even our four year old was throwing ideas out there. We all agreed and disagreed on many things. It was a good, fun day activity. It took hours. We had a buffet lunch, in the middle, as it took so long. When you've got that, it is so special and it is so powerful. The fact that you've all just sat around and listened to each other and felt heard, you all feel that strength and that bond in your family. It is unreal. This is one of the Days with us we offer families, **realign** with our one day course for families, come down connect and spend time with us. We create dream boards. You'll get heard. We all encourage you guys to do at least one dream on your pages, that if it doesn't scare you, make it bigger. We encourage you guys to get the best out of each other in a playful and uplifting way. We all get to share and then we help you guys to put that together on a family board and it's the most powerful, beautiful thing. It is so powerful. And it's so easy.

So, if you guys try this at home, and it doesn't work out for any reason, people aren't on board, you can't get them focused or for some reason you just can't get it all together on a family board, we offer a day's event where we, literally, help you guys with this. It's not some massive event with hundreds of people. We keep it to just a handful of families, just a few of you guys so we can do one-on-one, get in there with your families, make it fun, we make sure that you leave with that family dream board. So that you leave realigned. And really happy. It's such a powerful thing you will just love spending time with us and we would love to connect with you guys.

*"In every job that must be done, there is an element of fun. You find the fun and—snap!—the job's a game!"* – Mary Poppins

## Activities

All family members get their own piece of paper. Then write out five things for each category:

1. What they would love to do,
2. Where they would love to go and see,
3. What they would love to have,
4. Who they would love to meet.

It should take about 30 minutes to complete, really think, really go above and beyond and try to create a really amazing list.

When this has been completed by everyone, all come back together as a family. Now you're all going to talk about your lists. You take it in turns to share, one at a time, everyone **listens**.

Take notes if you need to, letting each person speak, one at a time, really listening to each other.

Once everyone has been heard, you can see if any of the lists overlap. If anyone has anything in common, or very similar goals, you can now see what you are all aiming for.

Now use the family goal sheet, again with the same four categories, decide on six things for each list. So now you've got your lists, What they would love to do, Where they would love to go and see, What they would love to have, and who they would love to meet.

Using the last A-1 piece of paper, from the Dream Board kit (these kits are available on the www.foreverfamilyforeverfree.com), put all of the items from the family goal sheet onto the A-1 Vision Board. Using the list you have created and by using as many pictures as possible. You can use travel brochures, catalogs, magazines, you can Google Image things and print them off, you can even draw them if you're creative, that's brilliant. You want this in colour, you want to make it as visual as possible. With all the family members taking part, really get everyone involved, this should be a really fun activity for the whole family.

Once you have completed it, hang it up to dry. When it's all dried, you need to hang it in a place where the whole family will see it every day.

Ours is in our bathroom, but you can have it on the living room door, you can have it in your bathroom, you can have it in the kitchen, the hallway, back of the front door, somewhere where you will all see it at least once a day.

*If you want extraordinary lives , the lives other people dream of, you've got to get out there. You've got to do things differently. You've got to stand out. Be prepared to be different if you want that different life.*

**Activity Two.**

For the next seven days, each family member, every morning, writes out five things that they are truly grateful for. (feel it guys)

Try and make these things different each and every day. After seven days, try and go for another 14 days, really think of what you're truly grateful for in your life. We have found it's impossible to be sad or depressed *and* grateful at the same time.

After 21 days of doing something consistently, you create a new habit. This will be a great new positive habit that will be formed. Continue with the gratitude list, thinking of five things daily, ideally in the morning. This way you set up your day to be a fun, and fulfilling day.

# Step Two
# Reconnect.

*"Family: A social unit where the father is concerned with parking space, the children with outer space, and the mother with closet space." » Evan Esar*

When we first had our children, we went from a couple to a family of four, in the deep end, we had crazy times. Those that know our story will appreciate the stress and trauma we were going through. We as the parents kind of lost our fun. We lost the cool, fun, "let's play with the kids" side of us for a little while, and on Tegan's adoption day we had a bouncy castle. And halfway through the party, we cleared all the kids off and we got all the adults on. I'm talking the aunties, the uncles, us, the grandparents. This poor, little eighty year old woman, bless her, she was loving it. She was all in, feet in the air, jumping up and down. And it really snapped us back to our fun selves again. Then that's when we realized that we'd missed that for a couple months. We'd lost our fun for a little while.

So, to reconnect, it's not just about reconnecting with your children. It's about reconnecting with the child within you. If you can go and find that fun place, you'll be amazed at how quickly you reconnect to your kids. So, we always suggest fun days Go somewhere, neutral but FUN! obviously, depending on how old your kids are, but you give them the control, the power, the kids RULE! "Okay, kids. Today is your day. We do what you say." So, to start with, you may feel a little bit out of your comfort zone. But, when you start letting go and just start being so silly and fun the reconnection you'll get with your kids in that short amount of time is priceless and it's brilliant. You look at the smiles on their faces. You take a moment, in that day, just to look and to see the bonds you create.

**What if I already have a good connection?**

Then that is awesome. Even with a great connection, would you pass at the opportunity to go and have fun with the kids? Come on. Go and do it anyway. Who doesn't love silly mummy and daddy doing crazy stuff? Even if it's just a day at the beach where you're the one that's buried in the sand and diving in and over the surfboards in the sea. There's no excuse not to be awesome and fun, Is there? Even if you've got a great connection, this is still fun to do.

**I don't have enough time.**

Family time. It doesn't have to be a today, it doesn't have to be right now. You can, literally, schedule it in. You'll find, once you've realigned, the free time you have at home won't be stressing at each other. It becomes more precious and more valuable. When you start living in the attitude of gratitude and really appreciating your family for who they are,  you'll find you have so much more time when you don't have a head full of stress. You can, literally, schedule time.

It doesn't have to be a whole day. It can be a few hours, here and there,  you don't even need to go out it could be a family dinner, just ensure you have fun. It may not seem like a lot, but you'll find that the more you do it, the more time you will find. I promise you.

**What if I find it hard to let go?**

*Olaf to Princess Anna, "Some people are worth melting for."*

So, if you find it hard to let go...............

**IT'S FOR YOUR KIDS!!**

It's not about you. Get out of yourself. It's not about you. It's about your kids and your family. Don't worry about what other people think, and if you're having that much of a hard time, travel. Go a bit further a field where you will not know anybody. If it's that much out of your comfort zone, do something fun and silly at home.

## IT'S FOR YOUR KIDS!!

Does anything else matter? Is there anything else that matters more? Is your pride more important than your kids? Is your ego more important than your relationship with your kids? You will not get this time back. Let it go, guys. Let it go.

### What if other family members do not want to join in?

This is where you have to take the lead, guys. You take them anyway. You have to go all out crazy. If you're playing at your top craziest, they will start to be drawn in. If you're playing all out crazy, full energy, their enthusiasm will pick up and pick up until they, eventually, match yours. If you do it half-hearted and they don't want to do it, you are not going to turn them around. You need to play all out, super crazy, wacky. Wear fancy dress. Get your face painted at the fun place. You need to go all in, guys, and, if you have too hard a time, again, get in touch with us. Let's connect. Let's make this happen.

So this chapter, guys, is all about creating magical moments. Memories that will last a lifetime. It's the silly, fun moments that we do crazy, outrageous things, that we really be our true selves that our children are going to remember. It's not the cool stuff we buy them. It's not what we can and can't afford. It's that precious time that we spend with our children. It's the magical moments that we create that make this relationship great, that make us reconnect, that lasts a lifetime. That's the things they remember. They won't remember their favorite computer game. They won't remember what toys they played with, what scores the games were. They will remember their precious moments with you.

We do this as a one or two day event where we go out and it's nothing but fun. So, the kids get to be captains of your teams. You have to do what they say. And we bring the energy. You will never be as crazy and out there as us. So, if you get even close, I promise you, your kids will never forget that experience. It is magical. Not only that, we have a photographer who captures some of these moments. So, you really can create a magic moment that lasts a lifetime.

*"You're mad. Bonkers. Off your head... but I'll tell you a secret... all of the best people are."*

*— The Mad Hatter, Alice in Wonderland*

**Activities**

Plan a family day where you can all get together. We know this can be hard, especially if you have older teenagers. But get a day that you can all be together, even if you've had to plan it now for four weeks ahead. If you cannot get your family all together for one day, then how bad do you really want to connect and succeed with your family?

Before the day arrives, you'll need to plan what you're going to do and where you're going to do it, and with this, try not to choose something that one person likes. Either try something you used to do as a family before, that you know you all like, or try something completely new that could be really great fun.

As an example, I'll tell you one of the things we have done. Bare in mind, our kids are younger. So you can go to a big soft play area. From the moment you get there, you announce the children are in charge. Yep, that's right. The kids are in charge, you have to do what they say. So after five minutes of feeling a bit silly, you forget all about that. You jump in, you join in, you go down the death slide, you jump in the ball pools, you climb the obstacle courses. It is awesome fun, the connection with your children is amazing.

So when the day starts, when you're at your destination, your children will take charge. So it will be up to them to choose who does what, and how we do it. Remember, it's fun. Release your inner child. Connect with your children by being that inner child again. Laugh. It's so important. Laugh. If things go really wrong, you have to laugh. That is just life, that's how we get through this thing called parenting. You can't take yourselves too seriously. Get out there, have a real giggle, bond with your kids, and most importantly, enjoy it. This is fun!

# Step Three

# Grow Together.

*"I have found the best way to give advice to your children is to find out what they want and then advise them to do it." »*

*Harry S. Truman*

So, this is going over a few things again and creating new habits. Setting life goals and having fun as a family. Getting them all aligned and heading in the same direction. It brings all three steps together, now, to make this magical, powerful family.

When we first did this, we all had a shared goal. (we are sure many of you have heard of Matt and Caleb Maddix.) On our dream board, we photoshoped (some would say it's almost stalkerish) our family photo with their faces in. We all had that same vision that one day we would meet these guys. We didn't know how. We were broke and lived in the UK. They were out there smashing it out in the US, touring the world, doing all these speaking events.

Two months after we put this on our dream boards, Team Maddix were coming to London for an event we were involved in and an event that Tegan was speaking at, she was sharing the stage with these guys, because we were part of the team, the organizers put it out there that these guys needed a lift back from the airport. Boom! It took me fourteen seconds to respond. We got Team Maddix. The end of that weekend, we shared with them our story about our dream boards. They really believe in the law of attraction. We even showed them a picture of our dream board with their faces on and rather than being freaked out, they were absolutely humbled by that. They helped us recreate that photo.

We had a photo that was on our dream board. It was one of our goals. It wasn't one of those, "Oh, that would be cool if that happened." As a family of four, we focused on that. We looked at that picture every day. We took the steps to make that happen. We had no idea how when we put that on the dream board, but we made that come to life. Not only did we make that happen, it was the most enjoyable weekend of our lives. It was, like, two weeks before Christmas. We didn't even have our decorations up when we got back. We weren't even bothered. Like, the kids didn't even care about their advent calendars. Nothing was as special as the weekend we got to share with some superstars. We spent that weekend with world changers, all because we'd actually aligned and focused on our goals.

**What do you mean "grow together?"**

So, this is where we bring the first two all together and really channel it. So, we've realigned. We get our dreams and goals set together. We work out how we're going to help each other. We also have dedicated family fun time. Even if you've got to schedule it in, you have that family fun time. As an extra step on growing together, you have time where you sit down as a whole family unit. This is where you have something you can hold. Whether it be the book that you're reading right now, a favorite Teddy, and whoever is holding it, gets to speak. So they get to tell you how their week has been, what they've loved about the week, all their best moments.

Then we also get deeper they ask the following question. They say, "Have I been a great dad this week? Rate me out of ten." "Have I been the best mum this week?" Brother, sister, whatever it is. We learned this from Darren Hardy's, "Compound Effect" This is something he does with his wife, then the conversation really starts flowing and you can all discuss how you can step up your game and always be improving. If you're always out to build that relationship, and make it better. It's always going to improve. If you get the little things out of the way, on a weekly basis, it just gets stronger and stronger. Rather than have the little niggles that eventually cause an argument, you clear the air and get it out there. You have to remember to take it in turns, keep going around until everyone has finished  and make sure everyone gets heard.

**Is family time still heartfelt if it's scheduled?**

Any family time is heartfelt. If you're that busy you've got to schedule it, your children now know that they are as important as that business meeting. They are as important as that business trip, that self-development event. They're just as important, if not more. You can schedule it, especially if you've got older kids, schedule it so all at the same time your iPhone's all beep, you all know, "Come to the table. It's family time, guys." Let's make this happen. Whatever it is. Just a family talk, one day, whether it's a family day out. Whether it's every Sunday. Guys, we're going to have a meal together. So, we'll all meet up at this time, we'll go to our favorite restaurant. We'll all sit around and have a laugh and have just a great time and share our week and our stories good and bad, just really keep that connection strong.

**What if we don't agree with others' goals and dreams?**

*"Unconditional love is loving your kids for who they are, not for what they do… it isn't something you will achieve every minute of every day. But it is the thought we must hold in our hearts every day." »*
*Stephanie Marston*

It's not whether we agree or whether we like them. It's the fact that we all listen, we all feel heard and we help them where we can. Unless it's something really unethical or dangerous, then, obviously, you need a deeper chat about that, but if it's just something minor, like you're someone who's very academic, as a parent, and the kid wants to be a musician or an actor or an artist. The world's changing, guys. You have to support that or maybe come to a compromise. You're happy they'll go for that if they keep their grades up in the subjects you feel are important, too. You're a family. You're a unit. You don't have to agree on everything. You've got to remember, underneath it all is unconditional love. You are family. It doesn't matter. Unconditional love wins above anything else that you agree on.

**How to be sure we've really listened to each other.**

This is why I suggest that you have something that you have as, like, a symbol. When someone's holding this symbol, our book is a great one because, hopefully, you guys have read it or you've attended a course, so, our faces are on the cover, a smiling reminder that you can have a awesome family too. So, someone holds this book and when they hold that book everyone else is quiet. Even if you're the parent whoever is holding that book, you have to let them be heard. It's so important. If the parents are getting all what they want to say out and the children aren't, you're back to square one. It's just so important. Everyone needs to be heard and you need to be in the moment. No phones. No computer. No social media. You be in the moment and you pay attention.

You need to go around that circle until everyone has been heard. You just keep going around until everyone's been heard, everyone's shared, everyone's answered any questions or quibbles that have come up in the conversation. You just keep going around so everyone gets their say, everything gets said, and nothing gets left to be dwelled on. Then it's all out there in the open.

**What if you don't enjoy the same activities?**

If you don't enjoy the same activities, find some new ones that you can enjoy. One of you likes rollerblading. One of you likes the cinema. Find something in the middle like bowling. So, it's not too out there, it's not too boring. It's something in the middle. You guys don't like the same things, how much fun is that going to be, going out exploring all new activities until you find something that you do enjoy? Just learning something new together will be such a giggle you'll forget why you're even doing it. It'll just be a blast. So, don't ever worry about not having the same interests.

**What if we don't like what we've just heard?**

Okay. So, sometimes when you're passing the book around and hear what others have to say about you, about issues they've had, it's not always going to be pretty. But, if it's out there, it's something you can work on and overcome. If they kept that inside, over time that would just grow and grow until they, eventually, forget why they don't like you, but there's a resentment there. So, even if you don't like it, it's good to hear it. If you don't know it, you can't fix it. So, even when you don't like it, it is so important to be quiet until it's your turn to speak and then you guys can work through that together. So, even if you don't like it, you have to follow the process. If you don't follow the process, this will not work.

*"Always kiss your children goodnight – even if they're already asleep."*

*H. Jackson Brown, Jr.*

**What if, what if, what if?....**
**Loads of reasons not to do this.**

There are loads of reasons not to do this, guys. There are so many reasons that you could make up. What if I don't have the time? What if it all goes wrong? What if I can't get everyone to sit down at the right time? What if I'm busy? What if the phone rings? What if? What if? There are hundreds of reasons to not follow through with this. There are hundreds of reasons to not take part, not put in the time, not put in the effort. There is only **ONE** reason to step up and make this happen, to do this and follow through. You either want to be a great parent and a strong family unit or you don't.

Now, we had children because we wanted children. We were going all out. We are going to be the best parents we can be. I will not rest until I have the title of "best mummy." David won't rest until he has the title of "best daddy." We are out there to be the best parents we can be.

Guys, we get one shot at this. One shot to be great parents. So that our kids can grow up and be the grownups that we are proud to call our children. We want them to be great people and when they come to their time to have children we want them to be awesome parents too. How do we do that, guys? We set the example. We need to make this happen. What we do speaks so much louder than what we say. We can say, "Yeah, yeah, yeah. We're going to do this. We're going to do this." If we don't take action and follow up on that, it doesn't matter what we said. You have one shot, guys. One reason to make this happen.

# *They are your biggest "WHY."*

# *They are your kids.*

## How will you feel, if you do this?

Guys, guys, guys. Look at our cheesy picture on the back cover, man. This isn't us just posing for some photo shoot. We live like this daily. We get out there. We share this stuff. We live this. We love this. There's nothing better than having that closeness, that bond, that powerful family unit. We didn't have it as kids. Both me and David have come from broken backgrounds and difficult upbringings. We've all faced challenges. Even Tegan's had challenge's that she's faced. Maybe that's what's made us so grateful and such a powerful family, because we appreciate each other every single day. When we hug our kids, we're the crazy people that hold them for that extra second and breathe it in and go, "Wow! This is a cuddle I will not get again." You have to appreciate your kids.

If you break through, if you follow this book step by step or if you come to all our events and see them all through to the end, I guarantee you, it's a guarantee, money-back guarantee, you will have such a strong family unit. You will be a Mum and Dad your children are proud of. Your Children will grow into the adults you can be proud of.

Together the love will be unconditional. It will be so strong. Your children will be able to go out into that world and face any challenge. They know they've got the support, of not just you guys, but of their siblings. They know they can come to you with any issue and together you guys will face it as a team. Seriously, this is life changing. I know it's simple. It's only three steps. But if you can work through it and you can do this with heart and you can really work at this you will acheive the family that you deserve. You go to self development events, you go to business courses, they go to school trips. You all put everything into your success and your work life. If you can put the same attention, and more, into this and get this right, your life is set up. You will have that family. If you do all this and follow through, One, Two, Three.

Take these three steps to your perfect family, guys.

Three steps to family.

*"Love your family. Spend time, be kind, and serve one another.*

*Make no room for regrets.*

*Tomorrow is not promised and today is short."*

**Activities**

Similar to the activities in Step One,

We want you guys to go away separately, and write down your goals.
Write this list for half an hour, but focus on your life goals. Not the fun, cool stuff you want to have, do, and see?

1. Write down what's important to you,
2. What change you want to make in the world.
3. What is it that you're going to achieve?

Remember guys, if it's not so big that it scares you and everyone does not think you're crazy, then you are **not** dreaming big enough.

When everyone has done this, again come together, one at a time, go through your list and read it out. Remember guys, if their dreams seem crazy to you, they are on the right track. So listen, attentively and intuitively, listen and take note of each other. All take this in turns, and again, see if any of them overlap. See if any of you have the same kind of dreams and desires in life, or want to achieve. Or see where you could work together at achieving similar things.

Doing this, will really get you back on track to start growing together as a family. That way you can create your family goal sheet.

Again, once this is done, see if you can create a huge goal sheet on a A-1 piece of paper with all your goals and destinations. Remember, if it doesn't scare you, you're not dreaming big enough. So if you have to go away individually, or if you have to come together to find a massive goal that scares you, that you can all work towards and achieve together.

Remember guys, if you shoot for the moon, even if you miss you'll end up amongst the stars.

Once this is all completed, again put it up somewhere where you will all see it every single day. It will be great to take pictures of these on your phones and devices because it's great to see these at least three times a day, so it's always in your mind. That way, you'll be attracting these things at such a powerful speed, you will find it crazy.

**Activity Two.**

Similar to the gratitude list, that you learned in Step 2, this is all about the family members. So you'll need your family sheets of gratitude.     ,
We do this after dinner, as we all have our evening meals together.

For each family member, you write three things down that you're truly grateful for. They don't have to be massive things, they can be really small things. But they need to be three things that are important to you, and about them and try and make them different every single day. The more we focus on the reasons we are grateful for those members of our family, the more this will attract great things to us. The more we will appreciate and respect our family members.

Take these three steps to your perfect family, guys.

# Three steps to family.

# ✱✱✱✱✱✱

# Bonus
# Section

# ✱✱✱✱✱✱

# Three Steps to Family

# Our Morning Routine.

- We wake up straight out of bed, to get that body moving.
- We all get a drink of water, the grown-ups have a pint each, the kids have a big glass each.
- We then run through our gratitude lists.
  We really feel it, we feel the gratitude.
- Look at our Why. The reason WHY we are doing all of this.
- We focus on our vision boards.
- Then we do the Tony Robbins Priming Exercise, which you can find more details on our site.
- When we've finished that, we do our affirmations. "I will." "I can." "I am." All the positive quotes that you need to get into your mind.
- We then exercise. The kids get on the trampoline for at least 10 minutes. We make sure that we're out of breath for a good 15 minutes.
- We then read through our to-do list.
- Then jump in a cold shower, to wake the whole body up. Then a warm / normal shower.
- Once refreshed and ready, we read a self development book for at least 15 minutes.

This takes about an hour. We do all this before we have breakfast.

**That is our morning routine.**

# What are we grateful for?

We are grateful for each other. This amazing connection we have within this partnership.

We are grateful for our awesome son, Tyler David, he brings us joy and love every single day. The most positive person we know.

We are grateful for our awesome daughter, Tegan Helen. She is such a strong and courageous little girl, who will make a difference in the world.

We are grateful for the books and resources available to us.

We are grateful for our health.

We are grateful for our knowledge. That there is a better way, and we learn more everyday.

We are grateful for the opportunities to change.

We are grateful for the love we receive from our children.

We are truly grateful that we are action-takers.

We are grateful for being the 0.01%.

# Our Evening Routine

After dinner, our evening routine with the children is, we get out our goal sheets. We write down three things we achieved today, three things we will achieve tomorrow, three things we're grateful for about each family member. We then write down the best moment that happened to us that day, and we share those moments and we feel the love from each other.

We then read the children books, sing to them and they listen to an audio when they go to sleep in the evenings.

When it comes to our evening routine, we write down all of our ideas and thoughts, and reflect on our day.

We read 30 mins of a self-development book or listen to an audio. We then listen to a hypnosis, or a meditation that we fall asleep to.

**This is our evening routine.**

## Three Steps to Family

We would like you as a family to think about your own morning routine. Each family is different, and there is no set way, but you do need to come up with one that is right for you, to give YOU and your family the best possible start.

This can depend on the age of your children, they may have school, preschool, or college. We have chosen to homeschool our children, so we have a more relaxed household, but we still ensure that we follow through with our morning routine.

One of the best books based on morning routines that we as a family have read is, The Miracle Morning by Hal Elrod. He breaks it down into six lifestyle habits,

1. Silence the art of meditation
2. Reading of self development books
3. Affirmation, repeating positive things to yourself
4. Visualization and dream boards
5. Journaling and writing down the amazing things that happens throughout the day
6. Exercise, the power to wealth is through your health.

If you find that your mornings are hectic and stressful, (ours are too at times,) get up earlier. It is such a great feeling, getting up at 4am and getting your goals done, before the rest of the "norm" are awake. It really gives you a sense of achievement. We are not saying you have to get up at 4am, before you throw the book in the bin. But, If you can get up just one hour earlier, earlier than you would normally get up, and do 10 minutes of each of the six habits, as listed above. and if you can do this for 7 days, we are sure that you will want to continue for another 14 days. This will turn your new routine into a habit. Yes it usually takes 21 days to form a new positive habit. So don't do it for 2 days and give up, if you need more inspiration go back to page 51 and read it again.

If you have got babies or toddlers it might be difficult to get them to sit in silence or to read a self development book, but they can join in with the exercise, visualising and you ask them about any awesome things that they have enjoyed.

With our morning routine, no-one forced it, Laura attended a Upw event, and when we came back she wrote out her new morning routine. The next day Laura was up at five, implementing her new routine. After a couple mornings David starting joining in, though his exercises where different. After about a week Tegan started joining in again her exercising was different as she used the trampoline. About a month after we had started this new routine even Tyler would join in. Not always everything, he is only four.

The point here is we have never told our kids that they have to do this in the mornings, we changed our routine and habits and they followed.

Another great habit we all highly recommend is. Drink water, plenty of water, bottled water is better than tap water, but stop drinking that coffee, cut out the coffee, cut out the caffeine, that you automatically grab to give yourselves a boost. Drink juice, freshly prepared juice, we have a nutri-bullet, we really enjoy preparing the fruit and vegetables as a family trying out new ideas, and blitzing them into a juice.

*"As a parent, what you do speaks SO much louder than anything you will ever say to your children."*

# Three Steps to Family

# About the Author

*We see ourselves as a true power couple.*
*Not just power in life, business and success.*
*Most importantly in family, As parents.*
*We go above and beyond to be the best parents that we can be.*

*We have faced many challenges, over the last five years, but as a family we have got through them all together. We always put a happy spin on things and we always keep things positive. We have taught our children to live the life of their dreams. We've taught them they can do anything, yet they understand that this comes at a cost. Of time, effort and energy.*

*They know to set goals and to stay focused, they know if they can do this they CAN achieve the life of their dreams. We are so happy and proud to be the parents of entrepreneurial, HAPPY, fun loving children, who are out there to make a difference in the world, rather than getting stuck in the system.*

*Our mission as a family is to get out there in the world and help other families remember how important family is, to realise and appreciate each other, that time is precious, and we only get one shot at this. Family is special!*

*We believe everyone should be focused on their family. We teach families to listen, communicate, understand and be heard. We're hoping everyone takes the time to read this book, connect with us and try out some of our activities and events.*

*We are so excited to connect with other families, help make families important again.*

*We want families to ReAlign ReConnect and Grow Together.*

Thank you so much for taking the time to read this book. We know your time is valuable and we don't take this lightly.

Make sure you don't either!

Now make sure you go ahead and DO the activities in this book, TAKE action on the content you have read!

Go out and use this great information that we have shared, if you would like more help and support then contact us, and we really look forward to connecting with you guys and seeing you at our next event.

# Connect with Us

youtube.com/forever-family-forever-free

facebook.com/foreverfamilyforeverfree

To guarantee your place at our next event visit us
at : www.foreverfamilyforeverfree.com

To book us to speak at your next event email us:
foreverfamilyforeverfree@gmail.com

# Three Steps to Family

**Book  Us to speak at your next event.**

Book us to speak at your event and we will guarantee to deliver an incredibly **INSPIRING**, highly **ENTERTAINING** and truly **LIFE CHANGING** experience for everyone in attendance.
Our unique style combines, inspiring audiences with our unbelievable true stories,
keeping them engaged with our high energy delivery, And **EMPOWERING** them with actionable strategies to take their **RESULTS** to the next level.

We cover many family topics,

- How to have a happy home
- How to appreciate each other more,
- How to communicate more effectively.
- How to create more magic moments.
- How to create routines for winners.
- How to have strong bonds to become an unstoppable and powerful family!

Would you like us to bring some heart to your next event?

**Realign, Reconnect, Grow together.     74**

Whether you would like to book a workshop or a talk please use the form below to get in touch.

We also do workshops:

- ReAlign
- ReConnect
- Family Goal settings

Any queries please get in touch.

To book us to speak at your next event email us:
foreverfamilyforeverfree@gmail.com

We look forward to connecting with you.

# Three Steps to Family

# Three Steps to Family

20187751R00045

Printed in Great Britain
by Amazon